Family Walks
in West London

Caroline Bacon

Scarthin Books of Cromford
Derbyshire
1994

Family Walks Series

The Country Code

Guard against all risk of fire
Fasten all gates
Keep your dogs under proper control
Keep to public paths across farmland
Avoid damaging fences, hedges and walls
Leave no litter
Safeguard water supplies
Make no unnecessary noise
Protect wildlife, plants and trees
Go carefully along country roads
Respect the life of the countryside

Published 1994

Phototypesetting by Paragon Typesetters, Queensferry, Clwyd

Printed by Redwood Books Limited

ISBN 0 907758 72 X

Cover illustration by Ron Muschamp

The first Woodland Garden (route 4)

Dedication

For Dad

Preface

When it was suggested to me that I write a book of walks in the West London area I baulked at the idea. Surely, when people want a pleasant walk they go as far away from London as they can – to the 'real' countryside. But as I explored the area round my suburban home I realised that the outskirts of London hide many pockets of untouched landscape: ancient farmland, parklands unchanged for four hundred years, rivers and canals with ribbons of green to delight the walker all the more by their unexpectedness. Most exciting of all was the rich variety of wildlife to be found in these oases of countryside. Hobbies and sparrowhawks, myriads of rare insects and plants, all to be found within a short drive from the centre of London! I hope, therefore, that as you explore these walks, you too will be surprised and delighted as you discover the hidden secrets of London's green spaces.

About the author

Caroline Bacon was born and brought up in Northumberland, but now lives with her husband David and children Andrew and Rosemary in West London. She and her family are keen walkers and share a love of the countryside. Caroline is a freelance writer and has written a number of articles, including a series for the walking magazine *Out and About*.

Acknowledgements

My thanks go to Ruth Burton from Darley Dale in Derbyshire who produced the sketches that illustrate some of the walks. I am grateful also to the National Trust and the Crown Estate Office at Windsor for permission to include sections of their land in some of the routes. Many rangers and wardens gave up their time to give me information and my thanks go to them, particularly to Jim Walker, Nature Conservation Officer in Ealing Borough. Last, but certainly not least, I am indebted to a vast army of friends and relatives who have tried out these walks and given me valuable help in amending them. And of those, special thanks go to my husband David and my children Andrew and Rosemary, without whose patience this book would not have been written.

Contents

Map of the area

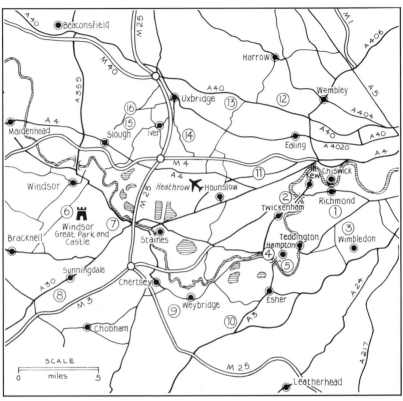

Paddington Arm of the Grand Union Canal (route 12)

Introduction

Families are the target of this book! And that includes anyone from nine months to ninety who likes to take their exercise in easy stages. In this collection of walks I have devised routes which are short, hopefully interesting and in some cases suitable for a pushchair. Some routes are only one and a half miles in length and the longest is only six. Wherever possible they pass at least one point of interest, be it a pond, memorial, or a playground, to give incentive to a flagging child. Despite widespread urbanisation, West London has a surprising number of green spaces. All of these walks are almost entirely 'rural', passing through fields, parkland and woods, only emerging briefly on to roads when unavoidable.

In each walk summary I have indicated whether it is suitable for a buggy. However, people vary widely in their opinion of where they can take a pushchair − narrow, overgrown paths may present no problem to one person, whereas to another they may seem impassable, even on foot! Only you know how you rate, so you must make up your mind using my comments as a guide.

West London offers a variety of scenery. A number of walks follow the towpaths of rivers and canals with their attendant narrow boats and sailing craft, or pass a lake where the enthusiast can enjoy the birdlife. Parkland abounds, a survival from the 16th and 17th centuries when acres of land were enclosed as royal hunting grounds. Often graced by herds of deer, this makes pleasant walking country with open space and fallen trees providing fun for the children. Scattered throughout are gardens of rhododendrons and azaleas − these are at their best in May and June. For those who like woodland, Black Park offers a forest of tall pines and in contrast Chobham Common is a relic of the open heathland that once covered much of southern England.

Choosing a walk

None of the walks in this book is difficult; there are no steep climbs to negotiate or rough moorland to cross. Nevertheless for young children the distance is all important − see how they manage with a short walk before attempting a longer trek. Always be prepared to change your plans − flexibility is essential. For this reason I have included a number of short cuts to give you that welcome way out when the burden of dragging a reluctant child round the complete circuit becomes unbearable.

Don't be deceived by the fact that you are in London. Paths can become overgrown and hidden in summer just as they can elsewhere and because of this some of the walks require greater concentration than others. On page 75 I have graded them according to length and difficulty. A canal walk is easier to follow than one through woods.

Allowing sufficient time

Some of the shorter routes can be completed easily in half a day, but a whole day is often more appropriate to allow times for rest, play and exploring. Be guided by the children and if you only get fifty yards from the car because they have found something to play with, don't feel you've failed. If the children have enjoyed themselves they will want to come back another day and you may be able to persuade them to go further next time. A pace of one mile an hour is suitable for very young children, while two miles an hour is appropriate for a ten-year-old.

What to wear

Walking, be it round London or in the heart of the Lake District, is always more comfortable if you wear strong shoes or walking boots. These are preferable to wellington boots on all but the shortest of walks. You may not need a compass, but the weather can be unpredictable in London just as it is on the moors! Waterproof cagoules are useful and remember warm gloves, hats and scarves in cold weather — nothing detracts more from a walk than a child who complains constantly that he is freezing to death! Include in your rucksack, as well as your picnic, plenty of tempting snacks and drinks for the children. You may like to take a couple of small handbooks on wild flowers or birds to help you identify those mentioned in the text — and in the autumn a container to collect blackberries.

Finding the way

All the walks can be found on the Ordnance Survey 1:50,000 sheet 176: West London, and this, in conjunction with a London street map will enable you to find your starting point. For the routes themselves you may like to take the relevant 1:25,000 Pathfinder sheets which are listed on pae 75 at the back of the book.

Refreshments

One of the advantages of walking near a built-up area is the number of eating places en route. Having said that, some of the walks defy this rule and have only excellent picnic spots to offer. Many of the pubs welcome children and there are kiosks or cafes, often open until 6.00 pm in the summer months.

Public transport

Bus, train and underground details are included at the end of each walk where appropriate.

Country Code

Even on the edge of London, the Country Code still applies. It is useful to teach children at an early age to have respect for the countryside and you will find the Code printed at the front of the book. Remember — leave nothing but footprints, take nothing but memories!

River Wey and the Wey Navigation (route 9)

Map Key

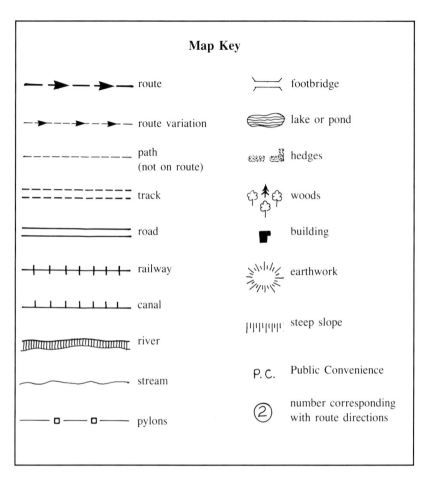

- ➤ ➤ route
- ➤ ➤ route variation
- path (not on route)
- track
- road
- railway
- canal
- river
- stream
- ⊡ ⊡ pylons

- footbridge
- lake or pond
- hedges
- woods
- building
- earthwork
- steep slope
- P.C. Public Convenience
- ② number corresponding with route directions

Nuthatch
Sitta europaea

Richmond Park

Outline
Pen Ponds — Pembroke Lodge — Petersham Park — Isabella Plantation —
Pen Ponds.

Summary
An open walk with plenty of space for children to run about and picnic as well as fallen
trees to climb on and a number of ponds with hungry ducks to feed, not to mention
the squirrels in Pembroke Lodge. The latter are fussy and will only eat peanuts, so
come prepared. This is a particularly attractive walk in late spring when the
rhododendrons and azaleas in the Isabella Plantation are spectacular. The shorter
version may be suitable for intrepid pushchair owners.

Attractions
Richmond Park must be the most famous of all London's suburban parks, and we owe
the privilege of walking in it to Edward VII who declared it a public place at the
beginning of this century. It was not always so. Charles I enclosed the land in 1637
against much opposition and in the mid-18th century when Countess Ameiia was
Deputy Ranger she seemed determined to exclude all but a few friends from enjoying
the Park. Tickets had to be bought to enter, and it was only through the efforts of a
local brewer, John Lewis, that public rights were retained. This brave man brought
a case against a certain gate keeper, claiming she had assaulted him as he tried to enter
the Park. Lewis won the case and a ladder stile was erected over the wall. Even so,
Countess Amelia made sure that the rungs were so wide apart that old people and
children were not able to climb over. Lewis protested, and the stile was remade.

Pen Ponds were made from old gravel pits in the 18th century and a number of
fish live in the water, including gudgeon, perch and tench and recently gamekeepers
found a huge pike which had choked to death trying to eat a bird!

Queen Victoria granted her Prime Minister, Lord John Russell, lifetime tenancy
of Pembroke Lodge in gratitude for services rendered. Lord John's grandson,
Bertrand, spent some of his youth here. To the right of the Lodge is Henry's Mound,
a burial mound that contained ashes when it was opened in 1835, but known as the
spot where Henry VIII stood to look for a signal to tell him that Anne Boleyn had been
beheaded.

Petersham Park, once a densely wooded escarpment, is a pleasant play area for
children. In the last century hundreds of children from inner London came here to
enjoy a day in the 'country'. The peculiar mounds on the slope are anthills, not
molehills, as there are no moles in the Park.

The Isabella Plantation is beautiful in May and June when the rhododendrons and
azaleas are a blaze of colour.

Route 1

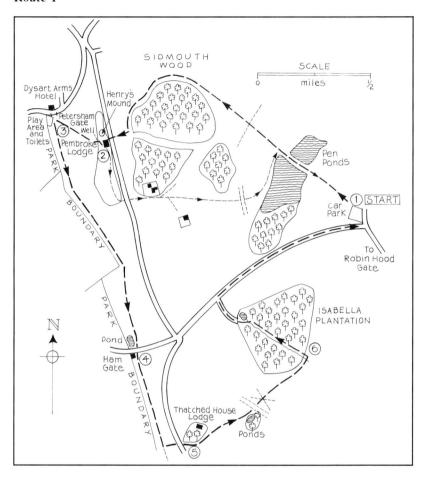

Route 1

Richmond Park

5 miles (Shorter variation 2½ miles)

Start

At Pen Ponds' car park. Where the A308 (Kingston Vale) joins the A3 (Roehampton Vale) turn left into Richmond Park at Robin Hood Gate. Go straight ahead at the roundabout, following the sign to Pen Ponds (GR 204726).

Route

1. *Follow the main path towards Pen Ponds, then walk between the Ponds and keep straight ahead with Sidmouth Wood on the left. Cross a path and follow the edge of Sidmouth Wood round to the left, until you reach a metal gate. Take a right fork here towards the road. Cross the road to Pembroke Lodge where there are toilets and a cafe.*

2. *Go to the patio area at the back of the Lodge and, looking downhill towards the river, turn right along the main path. Just before Henry's Mound rises up ahead, turn left downhill for 10 metres to a metal gate in the fence. Go half-right down a grassy track to Petersham Gate where there are toilets and a children's play area.*

3. *Turn left by two conifers and follow the footpath south, parallel to the Park boundary. Where a green field opens up on the right continue straight ahead on the path. Pass a pond on your right and cross the road beside Ham Gate.*

4. *Follow the boundary, choosing a broad path 50 metres from the wall. Just beyond the second estate of new houses that overlook the Park and just before the footpath goes up a slope, turn left and climb the hillside. There is no path so head towards a wooded area enclosing the Thatched House Lodge.*

5. *Cross the road and walk uphill with the fence on your left. At the top go across the road to a path with birch trees to the right. Continue past a reed bed on the right and then a fenced wood. Maintain direction uphill across a bridle track. At the top of the hill where six paths meet take the third left which takes you half-left downhill for 100 metres to a wooden fence. Bear right with the fence on your left. It joins the perimeter of the Isabella Plantation which you enter by the first entrance on your left.*

6. *Inside the Plantation take a left fork after 40 metres to reach a stream. Turn right without crossing the stream and follow it through the Plantation to a lake. Turn left over a bridge and leave by the gate beyond the lake. Follow the road to a junction, turn right and follow the road back to the car park.*

Shorter variation 2½ miles

At Pembroke Lodge, 2 above, turn left at the patio and walk to the end of the main lawn. Go straight ahead along a gravel path and out through a metal gate. Turn left and cross the road on to a made up path. Follow this until it turns left into some buildings. Walk straight ahead on the right-hand path of two main paths, ignoring a right fork that leaves after a short distance. Continue straight ahead through the trees, cross a bridle track and continue to Pen Ponds, joining the track that passes between them. Retrace your steps to the car park.

Public Transport

Bus routes 265 Putney Bridge Station to Tolworth and K6 Ham to Roehampton Vale pass the Robin Hood Gate. The nearest British Rail station is one and a half miles away at Norbiton — you join the walk at 5.

Refreshments

Pembroke Lodge serves snacks and cooked meals and the Dysart Arms Hotel is a popular hostelry by Petersham Gate.

Feeding the birds on Pen Ponds

14

Marble Hill Park, Ham Lands and the Thames

Outline

Marble Hill Park − Ham House − Teddington Lock − Ham Lands − Richmond −
Marble Hill Park.

Summary

A river walk combined with open space and views unrivalled in Greater London
makes this a delightful route. Children permitting, there are two stately homes to visit,
and, most popular of all, a ferry ride across the Thames. The shorter walk is suitable
for pushchairs.

Attractions

Marble Hill House was built in the 1720s for Henrietta Howard, the Countess of
Suffolk and mistress of George II. This elegant building, whose spacious grounds are
occasionally used for open air plays and concerts, is worth a look and entrance is free.
You may prefer to go into Ham House, however, once you have crossed the river.
The original ferry was a mahogany punt; today the craft is engine-powered.

Ham House was built in 1610 by Sir Thomas Vavasour before becoming the
property of the Dysart family, who made a number of alterations in the latter part of
the 16th century. The gardens with their formal hedges are a favourite with children
who love to play hide and seek, and there is an excellent tea room in the summer
months (see page 18).

Landwards of the towpath as you walk towards Teddington Lock is an area of
ground known as Ham Lands. Flint implements and Roman artefacts have been
discovered, but as the land was often flooded it is unlikely that people lived here
permanently. It was used for grazing until the early 20th century when it was
excavated for sand and gravel. These old workings have been filled in and now the
area is especially rich in plant life − if you are sharp-eyed you may spot bee orchids.
Stonechats breed here too, a rare occurrence in London.

As you walk towards Richmond enjoy the sight of cows grazing on Petersham
meadows, overlooked by the wooded slopes of Petersham Common. The wall
between the towpath and the field was built to stop the land from flooding − until
then locals used the frozen water in winter for skating! Occasionally at high tide the
towpath still floods − should this be the case you can follow the alternative route
across Petersham Meadows.

Richmond has a fascinating history, having been home to kings and queens
over the centuries and its architecture reflects its royal heritage. To know more
about the town, follow the towpath under the bridge, which was built in 1777,
and then walk up into the new riverside development to the tourist office − and coffee
shop!

Route 2

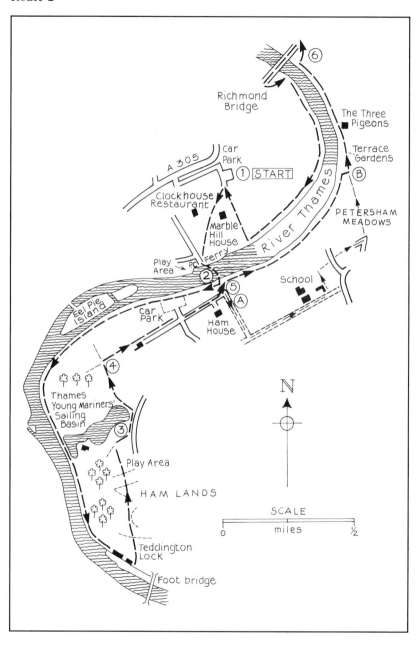

Route 2

Marble Hill Park, Ham Lands and the Thames   6 miles
(Shorter variation 3 miles)

Start

At Marble Hill car park, between Twickenham and Richmond on the A305 (Richmond Road, Twickenham). Going east the entrance is a small right turning 100 metres after Montpelier Row and almost opposite Sandycombe Road. The drive leads to the car park (GR 174738). NB If the towpath is flooded use alternative route — see page 18.

Route

1. *Looking towards the river, leave the car park and walk diagonally right across the grass between Marble Hill House and the Clockhouse Restaurant. Turn left between two fenced off areas and walk across the playing field towards the river. Leave the field by a gate on the right and turn left to Hammerton's ferry, passing a children's play park and toilets on the right. Take the ferry across the river. (This service runs from 10.00 am – 6.00 pm except Christmas Day. Tel: 081 892 9620.)*

2. *Once across the river, turn right along the towpath and walk to Teddington Lock. Just beyond the Lock Keeper's cottage take the first path on the left, continue across a minor footpath, then follow the path ahead which veers left. Cross a gravel path and continue straight ahead. Where another path joins and leaves on the right, keep left. After a further 50 metres where the path forks keep right, and then cross over two paths, walking straight ahead between brambles.*

3. *Where you reach a clear path, just before the Thames Young Mariner's Sailing Basin, turn right and continue past a children's play area to the road. Turn left past the entrance to the Sailing Basin, and then left back into Ham Lands, keeping the fence on your left. Where the fence ends, keep straight on ignoring all other possibilities until you reach a crossing path.*

4. *Turn right here and keep straight ahead until you come out at a playing field. Turn right along a path round the edge of the field to a road. Cross and walk straight ahead past the main entrance of Ham House.*

5. *A Turn half-left across the field to the river and follow the towpath right towards Richmond. Where there is a break in the towpath, turn right along a tarmac path and then left at B through some gardens (where you can follow signs to the Terrace Gardens) before rejoining the river.*

6. *Cross the river at Richmond Bridge, then turn left on to the towpath on the other side. Follow the river back to Marble Hill Park, turning right at the tarmac path that takes you to the car park.*

Shorter variation

Where the ferry lands take the towpath straight into Richmond. This version is suitable for pushchairs, provided they can be folded to accommodate the ferry.

Alternative route in the event of tidal flooding

Follow the tarmac path at A round to keep Ham House on your right and fields on your left. When you meet a track turn left, eventually crossing a road, and 80 metres before the main road turn left to cross a drive and take the footpath opposite. After 200 metres turn right between high wooden fences, cross a lane and walk between brick walls, coming out at a garden centre on your right. Follow the lane and where it turns right go left along a hedged path. Continue across Petersham Meadows to join the route at the riverside gardens, B.

Public Transport

There are frequent buses along the A305 including 33 Hammersmith to Fulwell Garage; 90 Richmond to Northolt Station; 290 Hammersmith to Staines; R68 Richmond to Hampton Court Station; R70 Richmond to Hanworth. The nearest British Rail station is half a mile away at St Margarets.

Refreshments

The Clock House Restaurant in Marble Hill Park is open in summer and Ham House has a tea room (081 940 1950). The Terrace Gardens has snacks and there are many riverside cafes and kiosks.

Hammerton's Ferry

18

Wimbledon Common

Outline

Windmill car park − Caesar's Well − War Memorial − Queen's Mere − Windmill car park.

Summary

Wimbledon Common offers a good mixture of open space and trees so that children can run about and explore without being too restricted to paths. It is possible for the very determined to take a pushchair although some parts are very heavy going.

Outline

Like all common land, Wimbledon Common was too poor for intensive farming and so it was grazed by animals and local people took wood for fires and dug out gravel and sand for building. In 1864 the Lord of the Manor, Earl Spencer, attempted to enclose the Common but, fortunately for us, Henry Peek set up a committee to fight the proposed bill. Terms were agreed at a cost which was paid by levying taxes from those who lived within three quarters of a mile of the Common. Until recently, local residents used to walk up to the Manor Cottage once a year to pay their dues; now the payments are included in local taxes.

The famous Windmill (which now houses a museum) was built in 1817 and in 1860, when the mill was no longer in use, the lower floors were converted into cottages. One former occupant of the mill, Thomas Dann, combined his duties as miller with those of constable and he had to keep watch from the roof not only for thieves but also for duellists.

As a secluded open space within easy reach of London, duels were frequently fought on Wimbledon Common. One famous meeting took place between the Prime Minister, William Pitt and a Mr Tierney, who felt that he had been insulted in the House of Commons. Neither party was hurt.

A different kind of shooting took place when the National Rifle Association chose Wimbledon Common as the location for its annual meeting. Incidentally, in 1874, Charterhouse School entered a team for the Public Schools' match and among the boys was a certain R.S.S. Baden-Powell, who, years later, was to write his famous *Scouting for Boys* in the Windmill itself.

You may like to make a detour to Caesar's Camp, an Iron Age fort from the third century BC and now part of a golf course. Excavations show it once had extensive ramparts and a timber stockade, but it is very subdued today. Caesar's Well, like the Camp, has nothing to do with Caesar! The granite slab circle laid in 1872 by Henry Peek marks the site of the well, which is now filled in, but if you walk a few yards downhill you will see one of the many local springs bubbling up into a trough.

For variety, the walk goes across the playing field where children can run about or kick a football, and passes the War Memorial with its copse of oak trees.

Route 3

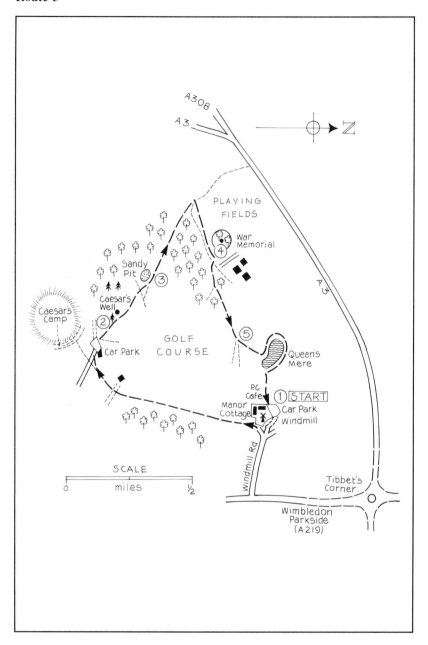

Route 3

Wimbledon Common   3 miles

Start

At the Windmill car park. From Central London turn left off the A3 at Tibbet's Corner along the A219 (Wimbledon Parkside). Turn right along Windmill Road and follow the blue painted signs to the London Scottish Golf Club (GR 230725).

Route

1. *Retrace your route out of the car park and turn right along a wide gravelled path, passing Manor Cottage on the right. Keep to this path for ¾ mile, passing a cottage on the right where you cross a bridle track and eventually emerging on to a road. (To visit Caesar's Camp cross the road and go straight ahead over the golf course. Turn left at a track and then take a right turn across the Camp. Retrace your route back to the road and turn left to the car park.) Otherwise turn right and pass a white one-storey building on your right to enter a small car park.*

2. *Ignore the white gate with a gravelled track beyond it; instead turn half-right and leave the car park by the boundary logs. Go straight ahead to a fork and take the left-hand path. Head for the pine trees you can see straight ahead. At the trees stop to examine Caesar's Well in the dip to your left. Then continue in the same direction, taking a path that leads into the woods with two wooden seats and the golf course to the right. Cross a gravelly path and after ten metres turn left at another path, passing a fenced sandy area on your left.*

3. *Follow this broad path, until it ends at a junction. Turn right here, and then immediately left where the path forks. After 100 metres turn right into playing fields and follow the right-hand hedge across the fields to the War Memorial, where the children can play.*

4. *In the right-hand corner of the field, behind the memorial, turn right on to a path where you can see buildings to the left. Turn right and then immediately left into woods. After 50 metres turn left at the fork and follow the main path. Pass a large beech tree on the right and emerge at the golf course. Follow the main gravel path straight ahead, ignoring smaller paths to the right and left. Note the unusual beech tree on the left.*

5. *At a point where the path breaks into three, take the left-hand fork and follow it downhill to the water's edge. Then turn left and walk round the lake. To return to the car park turn half-left at the end of the lake and climb uphill, when the car park will come into view.*

Public Transport
Bus route 93 Putney Bridge Station to North Cheam goes along Wimbledon Parkside.

Refreshments
The cafe at the Windmill provides snacks and there are excellent places for a picnic.

The Windmill on Wimbledon Common

22

Bushy Park and the Woodland Gardens

Outline
Cobbler's Walk car park − Woodland Gardens − Bushy Park − car park.

Summary
Bushy Park, although less well known than its counterpart in Richmond, is nevertheless an area of extensive parkland and it boasts two fine ornamental gardens. This
walk encompasses these and explores the west end of the Park. The shorter version
is suitable for pushchairs. Dogs are not allowed in the Woodland Gardens.

Attractions
300 acres of land were enclosed as early as the 15th century, but most of the Park
was created by Cardinal Wolsey, and completed by Henry VIII when Wolsey fell
from grace. For hunting purposes the King introduced fallow deer and there are 200
to this day. In addition there are 125 red deer and until ten years ago cattle were
grazed in some parts. The fine avenues of trees were planted in the 17th century when
the parkland was considered an appropriate adjunct to the formal gardens of Hampton
Court Palace.

A more recent addition has been the creation of the Woodland Gardens in the
1920s. They have a fine collection of shrubs, at their most magnificent in May when
the rhododendrons and azaleas are in bloom. On the first lake you come to you will
find a motley collection of goslings, ducklings and moorhen chicks in early summer,
always popular with the children. By the Waterhouse pond is a garden boasting plants
from different parts of Canada such as fireweed and prairie lilies − as well as the
inevitable maple tree. The focus of this is a totem pole carved by an Indian artist,
Norman Tait, which was erected in 1992.

The footpath that you join as you re-enter Bushy Park has a very unusual history.
It gained its name from the determination of a local cobbler, Timothy Bennet, who,
when rights of way through the Park were closed by George II, approached the
Ranger, Lord Halifax, and demanded that they be opened again. He had seen people
trudging past his shop in Hampton Wick weary from following the 'hot sandy road'
round the edge of the Park. When he died two years later it was with the satisfaction
of knowing that his efforts had borne fruit and the paths had been reinstated.

Leaving Cobbler's Walk to those with pushchairs you cross meadows to reach the
perimeter wall. Look out for green woodpeckers, and on a quiet day you may see a
fox heading for one of the fenced plantations. Kingfishers have been spotted on the
quieter stretches of water, too. You may be surprised to hear the raucous screech of
rose ringed parakeets − escapees from captivity which have bred rather too
successfully in the wild!

Route 4

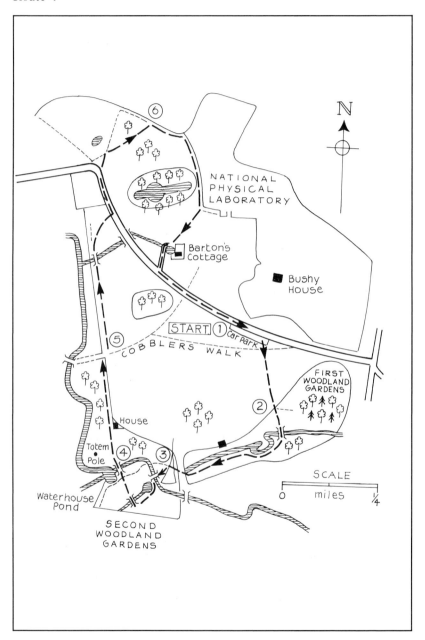

Route 4

Bushy Park and the Woodland Gardens

2½ miles
(Shorter variation 1½ miles)

Start

At Cobbler's Walk car park in Bushy Park. Turn left into Bushy Park from the B358 (Sandy Lane, Teddington and Kingston) from Kingston to Teddington. Take the first right turn which takes you to the car park (GR 155702).

Route

1. *Start at the south east corner of the car park by the map board and walk past a white barrier and bear slightly left across a path. Passing an oak on the left follow the grassy path until you reach a road. Opposite is a wooden gate into the first Woodland Gardens.*

2. *Once through the gate take the right fork and cross a wooden bridge. Turn right at a T-junction and follow the main path keeping the lake on your right. Continue past a cottage and through rhododendron bushes until you reach a gate. Go through it and straight ahead over a path to another wooden gate into the second Gardens.*

3. *Once inside take the first left-hand turn. Follow the winding path over a stream to a wooden bridge. Immediately after the bridge turn left and then follow the edge of the lake round to the right. Follow the stream, turn right over a small wooden bridge, and continue straight ahead with a stream on the left. Continue until you reach a waterfall and Waterhouse Pond.*

4. *Turn right and cross the stream keeping to the main path as it leaves the lake and passes through rhododendron bushes (noting the totem pole on the left). Pass a house on the right and continue down a broad grassy path with the perimeter fence on your right. At the end of the path go through a wooden gate and turn right through another gate into the main Park.*

5. *Turn immediately left and follow the fence until you pass to the left of a small canal. Just beyond this turn half-right across the grass to join the road. Turn left at the road and walk slightly uphill. When the road swings left, turn right along the first tarmac path and at a junction turn right. Continue to a metal gate out of the Park.*

6. *Turn right, following the path along the perimeter wall. Pass a long rectangular lake on the right and then continue along a tarmac path which swings right, with a football pitch on the right. Pass right of a pond and Barton's Cottage and continue to the road. Turn left here and return to the car park.*

Shorter variation

At 5 go straight ahead either following the tarmac path to the road and turning right or turning right after 100 metres along the grassy path called Cobbler's Walk.

Public Transport

Teddington British Rail station is a mile away. Bus route 592 Kingston to Stanwell passes the entrance to Bushy Park.

Refreshments

Occasionally in summer there is an ice cream van at the car park. Otherwise you can picnic in the Woodland Gardens.

Deer in Bushy Park

26

Hampton Court and the River Thames

Outline
Diana Fountain car park − Hampton Court Gardens − River Thames −
Home Park − Diana Fountain car park.

Summary
This walk takes you through the formal gardens of Hampton Court Palace and along
the towpath of the Thames to Kingston, ending with a pleasant walk through parkland
back to the Palace. As the towpath section is rather long, a popular short cut for
children involves taking the boat from Turks at Hampton Court Bridge to Kingston
Bridge, although this only operates in summer (see page 76). Pushchairs are possible,
if a little hard going through Home Park.

Attractions
As you leave the car park, persuading the children that they can play on the swings
on the way back, stop to admire the massive chestnut trees that line the avenue up
to the Diana Fountain. The Victorians had a celebration called Chestnut Sunday in
May, when the candles on the trees were at their most splendid, and this has recently
been reinstated by the Friends of Bushy Park.

Hampton Court needs no introduction. For those wanting more information the
kiosk on the left of the Lion Gate sells guide books and you can call in to see the 'real'
tennis court and the vine as you follow the route to the river. Children may like to
try out the maze on the return journey − if they are not worn out.

From Hampton Court to Kingston Bridge the towpath follows a loop of the river
and is bounded on the left by Home Park. The first section is very rural, in summer
the vegetation is lush with a profusion of wild flowers, including meadowsweet and
bugle, and alder and willow line the river bank. You may disturb a heron fishing and
there are rabbits in plenty.

After a brief return to modern life at Kingston Bridge where a constant flow of
traffic streams to and fro, Home Park offers a retreat back into the past. It was
primarily a preserve for deer and when Queen Elizabeth I came to hunt, the bells of
Kingston Parish Church would be rung in her honour. Not far from the entrance is
a red brick building, built in 1641 as an ice house to keep the venison cool. Ice was
carried by cart from Hampton Wick pond in winter.

On the left just out of view is the Long Water, part of an elaborate landscaping
scheme whereby avenues of trees were planted radiating from the central balcony of
the Palace in a vast fan with the canal as its spine. Some of this work was ordered
by William III who had the misfortune to fall when his horse, Sorrel, tripped on a
mole hill in Home Park. William broke his collar bone and died shortly afterwards
of a fever. The line of trees that this route follows was designed to line up with the
tower of Kingston Church.

Route 5

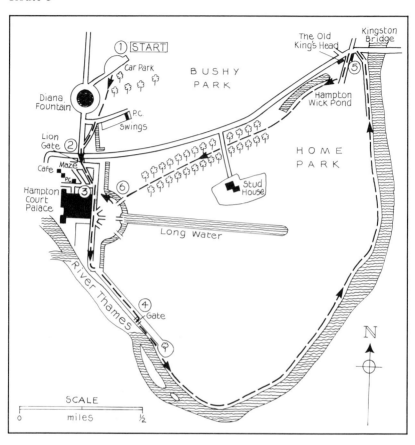

Kingfisher
Alcedo atthis

Route 5

Hampton Court and the River Thames   5 miles

Start

At the Diana Fountain car park in Bushy Park. Take the A308 from Kingston to Hampton Court (Hampton Court Road). Turn right into Bushy Park opposite the Lion Gate and the car park is on the right after the fountain (GR 161694).

Route

1. *From the car park walk towards the swings, passing to the right of them and following a track that goes half-right, at first with the canal on the left, towards the road exit of Bushy Park. Leave the Park by the iron gates and turn left to cross the main road by a zebra crossing.*

2. *Enter Hampton Court Palace gardens by the Lion Gate opposite. As you stand with the kiosk on your left take the second left path, which goes half-left towards a green door in a brick wall. If you want to make use of the toilets take the first left path, along a laburnum tunnel and follow the signs. For the maze take the right-hand path, following the hedge to the entrance.*

3. *Go through the green door and turn right along a broad gravel path passing the tennis court and the entrance to the apartments on the right. Continue past the palace and the vine entrance and follow a brick wall straight ahead until you reach a raised area overlooking the river. Turn left and follow a path beside another brick wall that runs parallel to the towpath. Continue until you reach a metal gate.*

4. *Go through the gate and down seven steps to the towpath and turn left. Keep on the towpath for 2½ miles until you reach Kingston Bridge. Walk up the hill on to the road by the bridge and turn left. On the left by The Old King's Head is an entrance to Home Park.*

5. *Walk into Home Park and immediately after the cattlegrid turn right over the grass to Hampton Wick pond. Keep the pond on your right and at the far end maintain direction to walk between an avenue of tall trees. Follow the avenue straight ahead until you reach the entrance to Hampton Court gardens.*

6. *Go through the gate and over a wooden bridge, then turn right and walk alongside the river. Turn left to reach the green gate in the wall that you came through earlier, and then turn half-right retracing your steps to the car park in Bushy Park. For the restaurant, cafe and maze follow the signpost as you come through the green gate.*

Public Transport
Bus routes 111, Kingston to Heathrow, and 216, Kingston to Staines, pass the Lion Gate. Hampton Court British Rail station is ½ mile away.

Refreshments
The car park has a snack bar and Hampton Court has a cafe and a restaurant as well as ice cream kiosks in summer.

The Copper Horse (route 6)

30

Windsor Great Park

Outline
Bishopsgate Road − Savill Garden − Obelisk − Smith's Lawn − Copper Horse −
Bishopsgate Road.

Summary
This walk begins with a rhododendron ride, beautiful in early summer, and passes the
famous Savill Garden. It skirts Smith's Lawn before crossing through wooded
parkland and fields to climb up to the Copper Horse with its magnificent view down
the Long Walk to Windsor Castle. Although there is a pushchair alternative, some
parts may still be hard going in wet weather.

Attractions
Windsor Great Park was so called to distinguish it from the 'Little Park' which
surrounded the castle. It was enclosed in 1086 and the Royal family of the day used
to stay in a moated manor house to hunt wild boar and deer. In those days there were
tracts of open land with marshes and streams and records tell us that beavers and
wolves were found there.

Because the forest is so ancient it is the habitat for a great variety of wildlife. Some
of the oaks date from 1580 when Elizabeth I ordered that more trees be planted to
replace those cut down to build ships for the Navy. All sorts of insects feed on oak
trees and 2,000 different kinds of beetle have been recorded in the Park. These in turn
attract birds, and you can see all three species of woodpecker as well as nuthatches
and treecreepers. Toadstools abound − see if you can find the sulphur-yellow
polypore, an orange fungus that grows on old tree trunks, or the bright red and white
fly agaric toadstool.

If you have time, the Savill Garden makes a delightful interlude. Started by Sir
Eric Savill in 1932, it has developed into one of the best gardens of its kind in Europe.
Beyond it is the Obelisk, built by George II in honour of his son, William, Duke of
Cumberland and on the far side of the Obelisk Pond is Smith's Lawn, reputedly named
after one of the Duke's grooms, Barnard Smith. Polo is played here regularly
throughout the summer − if you come at a weekend you may see a game in progress.

The enormous statue of George III, his hand pointing regally towards Windsor,
was commissioned by his son, George IV, who only lived long enough to see the
foundation stone laid. The statue itself, made by Sir Richard Westmacott, was erected
in 1831 after his death. It was so big that the truck carrying it overturned and the
horse's leg broke off! It had to be repaired on the slopes of Snow Hill and before it
was finally erected sixteen men climbed inside, ate their dinner and drank the health
of the King!

Continued on page 34

31

Route 6

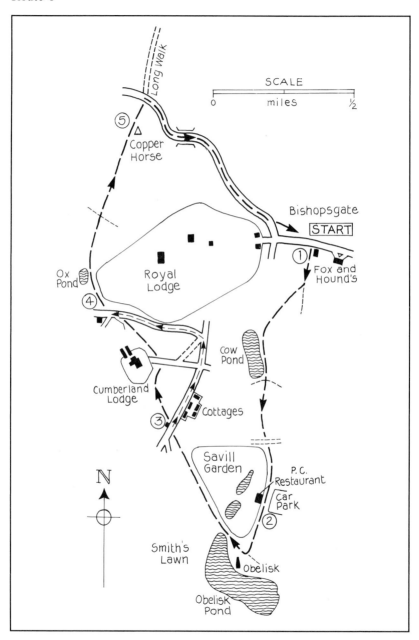

Route 6

Windsor Great Park

3½ miles
(Pushchair alternative)

Start

In Bishopsgate Road. From the A30 from Egham to Virginia Water turn right along the A328 through Englefield Green. Just before the Green itself turn left at the Barley Mow pub into Bishopsgate Road and continue to the Bishops Gate entrance to Windsor Great Park. There is parking space along the side of the road. Please note the Park Regulations posted at the entrance (GR 978722).

Route

1. *Go through the gates into Windsor Park and turn immediately left along a tarmac path past the Lodge. Go through a green wooden gate and continue along the path. At a fork keep right along a path lined with rhododendron bushes. Pass left of Cow Pond, go over a path and when you reach a tarmac path bear slightly left to go past the entrance to the Savill Garden with its restaurant, shop and toilets.*

2. *Follow the path to the Obelisk and turn sharply right downhill, leaving the tarmac path for a gravel one, and over a stone bridge. Continue straight ahead along a broad grassy ride until you reach a road.*

3. *Turn right through some gates and past a lodge on the left. **(Those with pushchairs see alternative route at end.)** Turn left in front of the lodge, leaving the road and walking through trees to a riding track by a fence. Turn right, following the route of the riding track, although not walking on it, until it joins a road. Turn left and after 20 metres right on to a path that goes half-left by a tree with a long overhanging bough. You pass tennis courts on your left and emerge at a junction of roads.*

4. *Turn left following a signpost that says 'Village Shop', but after 20 metres turn right, opposite the entrance to Chaplain's Lodge and follow a broad path downhill right of Ox Pond. Follow a grassy ride between hedges to the Copper Horse which you can see on top of the hill.*

5. *Walk downhill from the Copper Horse to the road and turn right. Follow this road round, through the deer gates and then turn left to reach the Bishops Gate entrance that you came in by.*

Pushchair alternative

At 3 pass the Lodge on your left but continue straight along the road. Pass a left-turn and after 200 metres take the right fork of two incoming left-hand tracks to re-join the walk at 4.

The climax of this walk must be the view from the Copper Horse to Windsor Castle. On a clear day you can see Heathrow Airport to the east and, with the help of binoculars, the tall buildings of central London. The Long Walk was begun in 1684 to link the Castle with the Park but, if you are considering a quick trip into Windsor, don't forget that it is three miles long!

Refreshments
The Savill Garden Restaurant is very good and is open most of the year (Tel 0784 432326). The Fox and Hounds is a popular pub in Bishopsgate Road but has few facilities for children.

Public Transport
Bus routes 441 and 443 Staines to Hedgerley stop in Englefield Green but there is a long walk down Bishopsgate Road.

Cooper's Hill woods

34

Runnymede and Cooper's Hill

Outline
Cooper's Hill − Runnymede − River Thames − Cooper's Hill.

Summary
A combination of woodland, open meadows and river makes this a varied walk and it has the added interest of three memorials commemorating very different events. There are plenty of refreshments en route and a play area, but this walk is not suitable for pushchairs.

Attractions
Either at the beginning or end of this walk you should visit the American Airforce Memorial and climb the tower to enjoy the view of Runnymede Meadows and the Thames. The Memorial was erected in 1949 in memory of 20,000 American servicemen who died during the Second World War and who have no known grave. Its monastic architecture and fresh white stone, coupled with the atmosphere of peace within it, make a lasting impression. Children are requested to be quiet.

The second memorial commemorates June 15, 1215, when King John, forced by a group of rebel barons, signed the document known as the Magna Carta (to distinguish it from other 'smaller' charters) which gave his noblemen the freedom to enjoy their land and properties without interference.

For those wanting to complete the trio, the third memorial is a block of Portland stone erected on land given by Britain to the United States to remember John F Kennedy who was assassinated in 1963.

The meadows at Egham were used as a race course from 1734 to 1884, which is why the land escaped enclosure during the nineteenth century. In 1860 plans were made to build a permanent grandstand, but it never materialised and now the only evidence of its existence are a few gaps in the hedges which mark the track.

As you go further downstream, the National Trust gives way to Runnymede Council pleasure grounds and there are seats facing the river as well as a children's play area. Just beside the modern bridge that carries the M25 over the Thames, archaeologists discovered evidence of a Bronze Age settlement and wharf. Among the fragments of pottery and metal work they found exotic ware from the continent suggesting that significant trading took place along the river.

A beaver bone was found during the dig and although you won't find any live specimens today, Runnymede is nevertheless a site of special scientific interest. By Langham Pond there are several unusual plants, including the greater water parsnip and the lesser marshwort as well as an amazing number of rare insects. Wetland birds, like the redshank, nest here, too. In the meadows you may see partridges, skylarks and corn buntings and there are nuthatches and sparrowhawks in the woods on Cooper's Hill.

Route 7

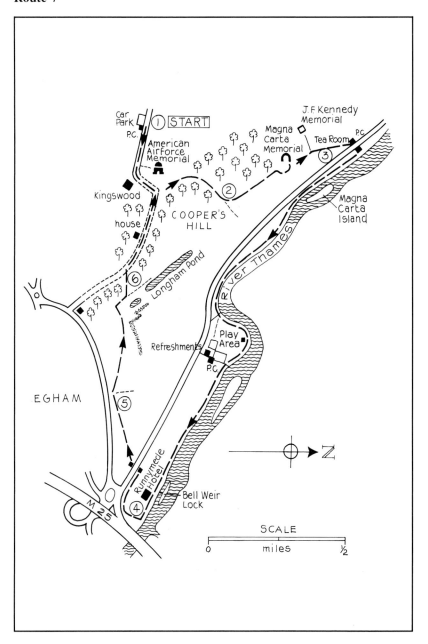

Route 7

Runnymede and Cooper's Hill   4½ miles

Start

> *At the car park in Cooper's Hill Lane. Turn left off the A308 from Egham to Windsor along the A328 (Priest Hill). Take the first left at the top of the hill into Cooper's Hill Lane and continue until you reach a car park on the right (GR 996718).*

Route

1. *Turn right out of the car park past toilets on the right and the Airforce Memorial on the left, which you can visit at this point if you wish. Pass Kingswood Hall of Residence on your right, continuing along the road, which soon degenerates into a track. Where the track goes right, take a footpath to the left into woods down a series of wooden steps. Follow it to a stile at the edge of the woods. Climb over the stile and go straight ahead with a line of trees on your right and a fence on your left.*

2. *Turn left over a stile just before the fence ahead and walk towards the Magna Carta Memorial, keeping the hedge on your right. Turn right over a stile and immediately left over another and left again to visit the Memorial. Continue (taking a detour into the woods on the left at the signpost to visit the John F Kennedy Memorial if you want), walking half-right across the fields to the two Lodge buildings where there is a tea room and toilets in the summer.*

3. *Cross the main road **carefully** (it can be extremely busy) and walk to the river. Turn right and follow the river bank, passing through the pleasure grounds with a car park, toilets and children's play area on the right. Continue along the towpath past houses on the right and Bell Weir Lock on the left to the Runnymede Hotel.*

4. *Just beyond the Hotel, but before the bridge over the river, turn right along a path which leads to the road. Turn right along the pavement and cross the road at the two small lodges. Walk across the meadows keeping the A30 on your left until you reach a tarmac path.*

5. *Turn half-right here towards the hedge that meanders across the meadow. Turn left to skirt a bog at the corner of the hedge and head towards the fence ahead. Turn right and continue with the fence on the left. Ignore a stile but instead go through a gate on the left 50 metres further on by an oak tree.*

6. *Walk uphill to a stile straight ahead. Climb over this into a track and turn right uphill, past a house on the left. This emerges at Kingswood Hall of Residence. Follow the road back to the car park.*

Public Transport
The nearest British Rail station is a mile away at Egham if you join the walk at 5. Bus routes 441 Staines to Hedgerley, P3 St Peter's (Chertsey) Hospital circular goes via Egham and the 718, London to Windsor operates in the summer only.

Refreshments
There are attractive picnic spots beside the river and the Magna Carta tea rooms and Runnymede Hotel both welcome children. A kiosk by the play area serves snacks.

Horse riding on Chobham Common

Chobham Common

Outline
Staple Hill car park − Albury Bottom − Chobham Common − car park.

Summary
From the raised site of the car park you can look south across Chobham Common at a vista that has been virtually unchanged for thousands of years. This walk explores the lowland heath now so rare in England, passing an Iron Age enclosure and wandering into the woodland that surrounds the Common to provide some shade on a hot day. The paths are good, but the thick sand in places makes it unsuitable for pushchairs.

Attractions
On June 14, 1853, Queen Victoria stood near to the present car park to review her troops who were preparing to fight in the Crimean War. For months beforehand sappers and miners had been digging trenches to house the kitchens. Rumour has it that during these preparations a certain quartermaster buried some barrels of molasses, hoping to keep them for himself, but local villagers heard about it and took to raiding the supply at night. When asked where they found it they would reply enigmatically that it came from the 'Treacle mines' on the Common.

The army has since settled in the locality, but not, fortunately, on Chobham Common, which is important for another reason. As one of the remaining areas of heathland in Britain, it is the habitat of many rare species. You may spot a hobby wheeling in the air − a spectacular bird of prey − and in spring and early summer take care not to disturb birds nesting in the heather. There are 300 different sorts of spider to be found here and half of all British dragonfly species live near the ponds. When you pass patches of wet heathland where there are pools of water, look out for fly-catching sundews and on dry sandy soil you may be lucky enough to see a lizard or a snake basking in the sun.

Heathland would have been familiar to early man as it was formed when the primaeval woodlands that grew on sandy soils were cleared and farmers grazed the land, using the heather and gorse for thatching and burning, and the birch trees for firewood. Today traditional land usage has changed and without careful management the heathland would revert to woods.

A reminder of the early days of the Common is found in the Iron Age enclosure known as the Bee Garden. It may have been a pound for animals, although its name suggests that it might actually have been used for beekeeping! Certainly the Domesday Book has a reference to a payment of £10 made to some monks for beeswax. Neolithic artefacts have been found within the enclosure, so keep your eyes skinned!

Route 8

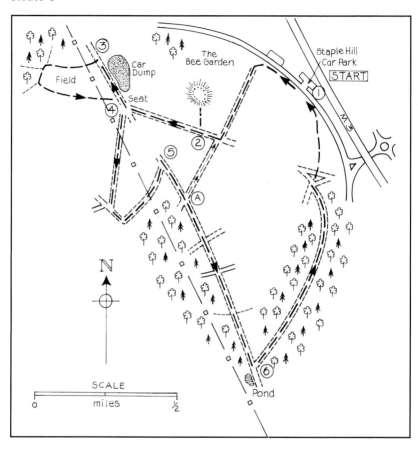

Common Sundew
DROSERA ROTUNDIFOLIA

Route 8

Chobham Common

4 miles (Shorter variation 3 miles)

Start

At Staple Hill car park. Leave the M3 at junction 3 and go south along the A322 towards Guildford. At the first roundabout turn left to Chobham along the A319. Turn left at the roundabout in the village and eventually take the first right-hand turn after the Cricketer's pub, which is Staple Hill Road. Stop in the second car park on the left (GR 973648).

Route

1. *From the car park cross the road and walk straight ahead between gorse bushes for 20 metres. Turn right when you meet the bridle path and continue until you reach an entrance to the Common on your right and a car park can be seen over the road. Turn left down the main path which soon broadens into a track. Where tracks cross turn right.*

2. *A few metres before a path comes in from the left take a right path at a post and follow it to a low mound just beyond another post, which is the outer rampart of an Iron Age enclosure. After you have explored this return to the main path (2), and turn right along it, ignoring minor paths to right and left. Ignore a major left-hand path and continue past two incoming right-hand paths, where there is a pond on the left in wet weather, and join a main track where you turn right. Ignore a left fork and continue straight ahead.*

3. *A few metres beyond a used car dump on the right turn left along a small path and go under the electricity cables. Follow a path with a field on the left. Turn left at a T-junction and keep left at each junction, eventually seeing the field again on your left. Continue under the cables and turn right at the track encountered earlier. Follow it for 100 metres to a wooden seat.*

4. *A few metres beyond the seat follow the second track on the right which swings right under the cables. Keep on the main track, ignoring any turnings off it until it meets a track. Turn left here and at a clearing follow the track round to the left and continue back under the electricity cables until you join a main path.*

5. *Turn right here and follow the track to a junction. **For the shortcut back to the car park, turn left here.** A. Otherwise, continue straight on keeping parallel to the electricity cables, and enter woodland. Ignore all other footpaths.*

6. *Just before a pond on the right take a left-hand track and follow it slightly uphill to where five tracks meet. Turn right and take the middle of the three paths ahead,*

to the left of some small conifers. Cross a main track and continue past a wooden barrier and go uphill, eventually joining a broad track. Go left and after 50 metres turn right to cross the road to the car park.

Shorter variation

At A, turn left and follow the track to join up with the route used on the outward journey. Retrace your steps to the car park.

Public Transport

The nearest British Rail station is a mile away at Longcross. There is an irregular bus service to Chobham.

Refreshments

The Cricketer's pub — or take a picnic.

Coxes Lock Mill on the Wey Navigation

River Wey and Wey Navigation

Outline
New Haw Lock − River Wey − Wey Navigation − Coxes Lock Mill −
New Haw Lock.

Summary
A mixed walk both through farmland and along the towpath of the Wey Navigation
which is owned by the National Trust. It can be muddy and as the towpath is very
narrow it is not suitable for pushchairs.

Attractions
You begin this walk by leaving New Haw Lock with its attractive 18th-century Lock
Keeper's cottage to follow a footpath across farmland that lies between the Wey
Navigation and the River Wey. Wey Manor Farm boasted fine sporting facilities at
the beginning of this century, including a polo ground, fives court and a cricket pitch.
For a time it became a golf course but is now arable and grazing land.

Cross the railway line with great care as it is unmanned. A scattering of one-storey
dwellings have been built on the other side of the line and there are a few houses on
the banks of the River Wey, but the land is unstable and has fortunately remained
undeveloped. A pond on the left of the river is all that remains of a large flooded gravel
pit, once a haven for birds; nevertheless you may still find a few ducks to feed, either
here or on the river.

At Town Bridge the River Wey and the Wey Navigation meet. It has always been
an important spot − neolithic tools suggest there was once a ford here, and the earliest
recorded bridge was built in 1571 for Queen Eliabeth I so that she could reach the
forest to hunt.

The Wey Navigation itself was constructed between 1651-53 by Sir Richard
Weston of Sutton Place in Guildford − one hundred years earlier than the Duke of
Bridgewater's canal which was supposedly the first to be built. It has twelve locks
along its 15½ mile length, stretching from Guildford to the Thames at Weybridge, and
it is now owned by the National Trust. You can get more information from their office
at Dapdune Wharf in Guildford. Corn, flour, timber, coal and many other goods were
carried on barges 72 feet long and 14 feet wide, and two of these retired boats are
moored by the bridge at New Haw.

You cannot fail to be impressed by the majesty of Coxes Lock Mill as you approach
it from the towpath. It is now converted into very desirable flats − if you can stand
the noise of the water − but it began life in the late 18th century as an iron mill owned
by a Mr Alexander Raby. He gained a reputation because he invented a water powered
hammer, known as 'Hackering Jack' which beat 2,700 blows an hour. His
inventiveness was his downfall, however, because his neighbour, the 'Bad Old

Continued on page 46

Route 9

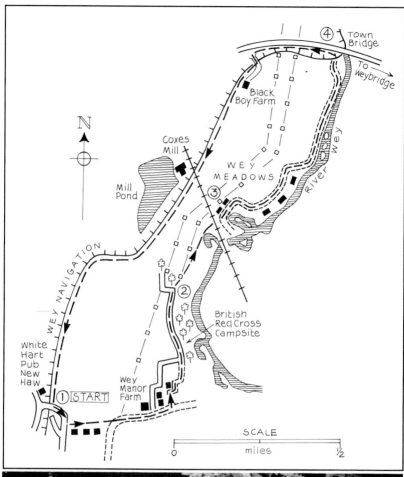

44

Route 9

River Wey and Wey Navigation   3 miles

Start

At New Haw Lock. Take the A317 from Weybridge to Chertsey and turn left along the B3121 signposted to Addleston. Continue for half a mile, first crossing the railway line, and then turn left along the A318 to Byfleet. Just past a roundabout the road crosses the canal at New Haw; a disused section of road on the right serves as a parking area (GR 056630).

Route

1. *From the parking area cross the road at the bridge and turn right along the footpath beside the road (not along the towpath). Just before some houses turn left along a signed footpath. When you join a wider track turn left. Turn left again at the next junction of paths, passing a farm on your left. Follow the farm road, eventually passing a British Red Cross campsite on the right.*

2. *Where the road turns left, follow a broad path straight ahead across an open field and underneath the electricity cables. Go over a stile with trees and a dried up oxbow lake on the right and after 70 metres climb over another stile. Continue to the railway line and **cross with care**.*

3. *Turn left along a track with bungalows on the left and continue, passing a number of plots of land and houses on the right. The route follows the River Wey and eventually emerges on to a road bridge over the canal.*

4. *Turn left to cross the canal and then go left to join the canal towpath. Turn right along this and cross the canal at the next bridge. This leads to Black Boy farm. Use the footbridge section which brings you out on to the towpath on the other side. Follow the towpath past Coxes Lock Mill and back to New Haw.*

Public Transport

Bus routes W3 Woking to Addleston; 427 Richmond to Addleston; 436 Heathrow to Guildford; 451 Staines to Kingston all pass New Haw. Byfleet and New Haw British Rail station is half a mile away.

Earl' of Portmore was so annoyed by the noise of the hammer that a feud arose and in 1808 Raby sold up and went to live in South Wales. The mill was converted to a corn mill and remained so until the end of the 1970s.

Look out for mimulus growing on the towpath with its bright yellow flowers in summer. Alder and willow grow by the canal, their roots helping to strengthen the banks. On the millpond at Coxes Lock there are coots and great crested grebe.

Refreshments
The White Hart pub at New Haw Lock and there are places to eat in Weybridge.

The pond at West End

46

West End and Esher Commons

Outline
Car park − West End Common − Esher Common − West End Village − car park.

Summary
The common lands near Esher are mixed woodland, making them particularly welcome on a hot day, but they are attractive at all times of the year. The route passes the pretty village of West End, where the Prince of Wales pub offers refreshments and facilities for children and Garsons 'Pick Your Own' farm provides a wide range of fruit and vegetables. Claremont Landscape Garden, owned by the National Trust, is well worth a visit.

Attractions
Common land was originally owned by the Lord of the Manor, who allowed his tenants to graze their livestock on it and to cut turf and collect firewood. As the soil is poor it was not enclosed for farming and it remained as heathland for hundreds of years as grazing animals prevented the invasion of trees. Then, in the 1830s, Scots pine was introduced and you can still see some of these original trees, especially on Esher Common. Many were cut down in the First World War and in their place grew deciduous trees such as oak, beech and silver birch. Tawny owls and sparrowhawks are among the birds that live here − the latter builds a new nest each year high up in a tree. You may catch sight of a treecreeper darting up a tree trunk searching for insects and see if you can spot wood ants' nests made from piles of pine needles.

There is a fine view in winter from the top of the Ledges over the River Mole and across the valley to Hersham. Bronze Age man liked this spot too: neolithic flint tools have been found here.

A pleasant resting place, despite the noise from traffic on the A3, is Black Pond, a small man-made lake where water was collected to serve Claremont House. You may be able to find the remains of a circular brick building (GR 129623) which was once a donkey-operated pump. Today the pond is mainly used by moorhens and herons and is fringed with reedmace.

It is hard to believe that a Mr Turner, in a book called *A Saunter Through Surrey* called West End 'a most marshy, stinking and choloric locality'! It would be hard to find a more picturesque green in West London and it is a good place for a picnic.

Refreshments
Garsons Farm Garden Centre has a restaurant which is open all day and serves hot meals between 12.00 noon and 2.00 pm (Tel 0372 460181) and the Prince of Wales pub welcomes children and has a garden.

Route 10

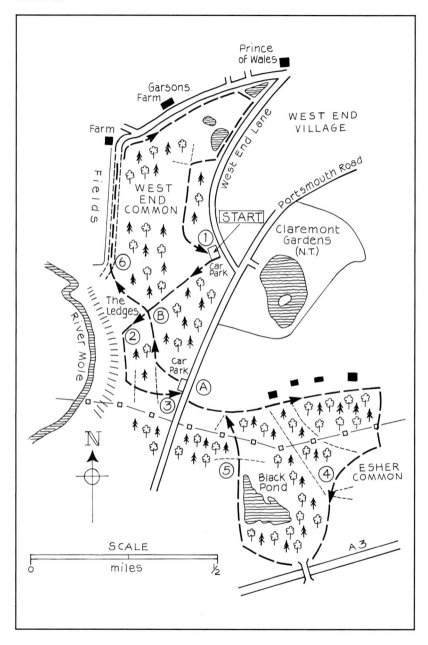

Route 10

West End and Esher Commons

4 miles (Shorter variation
2½ miles)

Start

At the car park in West End Lane. Take the A307 (Portsmouth Road) from Esher to Cobham and turn right opposite the entrance to Claremont Landscape Garden into West End Lane. The car park is 100 metres on the left (GR 126633).

Route

1. *Go through the wooden rails and take the left-hand fork. At the woods ignore a left fork and at a choice of three paths go right. At a clearing by a tree with four trunks, follow the main path left and go over a 'horse ride' **B** to take the right fork at a 'no horses' sign. After 20 metres turn left uphill and then take the right fork to the top.*

2. *Turn left along the ridge and, just before protective wooden rails on the right, turn left along a minor path, arriving after 50 metres at a copper beech tree. Continue over two crossing tracks to an open space. Go downhill to a car park.*

3. *Turn right along the main road and cross at the bus stop. Take the left path that follows the fence and where it divides into three, turn left along a bridle path. Continue to the third path on the right which is just beyond a house with a swimming pool in the garden and is opposite a gate with a 'Private' sign on it. Turn right here, and continue past wooden barriers and under electricity cables. After passing another wooden barrier turn right.*

4. *At the bottom of the hill, where five paths meet, take the third left walking to the right of a tree with a 'no fires' sign. This goes downhill and slightly right, becoming metalled where it passes a footbridge over the A3. Follow footpath signs to the Portsmouth Road, turning right at the second sign to walk along the edge of Black Pond.*

5. *Keep straight ahead, over a crossing track, under cables and over another track until you rejoin the route to reach the main road. Cross it, turn right and at the car park **A** take the right-hand gap in the wooden rails, then go uphill by the 'Common' sign. At a small clearing maintain direction through another clearing to a wooden barrier. Turn right on to a main track. At a meeting of several paths turn steeply left downhill, then turn left following the sign to Winterdown Road. Go over a crossing track **B** along a horse ride to a track by a field.*

6. *Turn right and follow the track for ¼ mile, eventually crossing the village green. Turn right across the green by the pond and keep the main road on your left.*

20 metres after a second pond turn right and then left after a small stone bridge over a stream. This path eventually veers left up wooden steps to open ground. Take the left fork back to the car park.

Shorter variation

*At 3 don't cross the Portsmouth Road but continue the walk as described from the car park **A** in 5. Or turn right along the horse ride at **B** and continue as for 6.*

Public Transport

The bus routes 510 and 415 from London to Guildford stop at Claremont Gardens.

GREY HERON
ARdea cineRea

Osterley Park

Outline

Osterley Park − Osterley Fields − Osterley Park.

Summary

This is a pleasant walk through fields that have been used as farm land for centuries and culminates in a tour of the delightful grounds of Osterley Park House. In wet weather the paths through the fields are extremely muddy. It is possible to take a pushchair through the Park itself.

Attractions

Osterley is first mentioned in the 13th century and means either a sheepfold clearing or western meadow, depending on which book you read. In those days wild cattle roamed the woods, which were the haunt of 'lawless men'. When the land was cultivated in the 14th century the quality of wheat grown was so good that it was baked into bread for the royal household.

By the 16th century the land had been given to local convents and when Henry VIII dissolved the monasteries it passed to Sir Thomas Gresham, founder of the Royal Exchange. It was he who built the original house and stable block in 1575. He also enclosed the Park, a most unpopular move, and during a visit by Elizabeth I, four local people pulled down the fences and made a bonfire of them − for which deed they were sent to Marshalsea jail. In the course of the same royal visit the Queen was said to have observed that a division of the courtyard in the house might improve its appearance. Sir Thomas secretly sent for workmen who built a wall during the night, and the Queen awoke next morning to find her wish had been carried out!

Numerous wildfowl live in Middle Lake at the eastern edge of the Estate, including tufted duck, pochard and great crested grebe. From the path that passes close to the water on the outside of the Park you may be rewarded by the sight of half a dozen herons perched on the branches of a tree on the island. In spring the gardeners (a misnomer!) help to ring the young herons in their nests high up in the trees.

As you enter the grounds, stop to admire a distant view of the House. It passed to the Child family in 1711 and was extensively altered by Robert Adam in the mid-18th century. Writing to the Countess of Upper Ossory in 1773, Horace Walpole considered the Park 'the ugliest spot of ground in the Universe', but he might have had a different opinion today. A number of ancient oak trees in the woods provide habitat for many different birds.

The large mound that rises up by the Garden Lake was an ice well, where ice was taken from the lake in winter and stored for use in the summer. On the left of the well the fenced tree is a cork oak, a mediterranean species whose bark is used to make corks for bottles.

Route 11

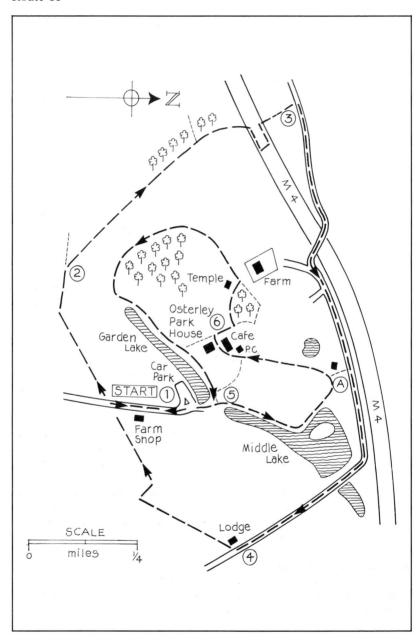

Route 11

Osterley Park

5½ miles (Shorter variations 3½ and 2 miles)

Start

In Osterley Park. From the A4 turn north into the B454 (Syon Lane, Southall and Isleworth), passing the Gillette Factory on your right. Take the first main left turning (Jersey Road) and after half a mile turn right into the drive to Osterley Park. The Park is owned by the National Trust and is open till 7.30 each day or sunset if earlier. There is a fee for the car park for non-National Trust members (GR 147778).

Route

1. *Retrace your route along the main drive and turn right through a metal gate just beyond the farm shop. Keeping the fence on your left go straight ahead towards the houses. Just before the road turn right, along the edge of the field, following the footpath sign to Heston. After passing through a hedge continue for 50 metres to a fork.*

2. *Take the right fork and follow the path, keeping the hedge on the right. At the end of the field, where the main path goes left keep straight on along a minor footpath and continue through a small wooded area towards the M4. Cross the motorway by the bridge and follow the path to the lane.*

3. *Turn right along the lane, cross the M4, and follow this road through some white metal gates, where it turns into a broad track. Pass the entrance to Osterley on your right **A** (entering the Park here if you wish to take a shorter route − see below) and follow the track round past the lake.*

4. *Just **beyond** the white Lodge turn right to a grassy area and keep right going through a gap in the wall to join a clear path which leads between fields back to the main drive. Turn right here and follow the road straight ahead into the Park.*

5. *Keeping the Garden Lake on your left turn right and follow a path round the edge of Middle Lake. By a small sign saying 'fishing permits only' walk half left to the green gate **A**, then turn left and follow Jubilee Drive past the toilets and the stable yard where there is a tea room.*

6. *Keeping the house on your left join a gravel path just beyond the house and turn right. Where this forks, turn left, and just past the little Temple of Pan turn left again. Follow this path round the perimeter of the Park. This eventually reaches the Garden Lake and returns you to the car park.*

Shorter variations

1. *At point* **A** *turn right in to Osterley Park and follow the track straight ahead past the toilets and stable yard, joining the walk at 6, a 3½ mile variation.*

2. *Alternatively you can start at 5 and do a shorter walk round the Park itself, a distance of 2 miles and suitable for pushchairs.*

Public Transport

The nearest Underground station is Osterley. Bus route H91 from Hounslow to Hammersmith goes to Osterley but not on Sundays.

Refreshments

From April to October the tea room is open from 11.30 am to 5.00 pm, except on Mondays and Tuesdays. There is plenty of space for picnics in the Park grounds.

On Horsenden Hill

Horsenden Hill and the Grand Union Canal

Outline
Horsenden Hill car park − Horsenden Farm Woods − Grand Union Canal −
Horsenden Woods − Horsenden Hill car park.

Summary
Rising out of an urban landscape, Horsenden Hill has apparently been bypassed by
the development that has taken place around it. On a fine day in summer the smell
of meadow grass and the sight of green hedgerows might deceive you into thinking
you are in the heart of the country. There are good paths throughout this walk
although wellingtons are advisable in wet weather, but it is not suitable for pushchairs.

Attractions
Horsenden Hill, derived from Old English words meaning 'horses' down', was
occupied in 7,000 BC by Neolithic people and archaeologists have found fragments
of flint and artefacts in the soil.

Although only 85m above sea level the views from the triangulation point are
impressive − if you have keen eyesight and a good imagination you should be able
to make out the Post Office Tower and St Paul's Cathedral to the east and the North
Downs to the south.

Look for small grassy mounds as you go downhill towards Horsenden Farm
Wood. These are the work of the meadow ant and are living colonies, so be careful
not to disturb them. During the summer the meadows are ablaze with wild flowers,
some of them rare in London, such as dyer's greenwood, so named because it
provided a green dye for cloth when mixed with the blue from woad.

In spite of its murky appearance the Grand Union Canal is the least polluted
waterway in the area, evidenced by the number of anglers along its banks, and if you
are fortunate you may see a heron fishing, or glimpse a kingfisher as it flashes by.
When this section of the canal was built in 1801 it was used primarily to carry hay
from the meadows of outer London into the city to feed the horses there. On the left
of the towpath just beyond the bridge is Perivale Wood, one of the oldest woodland
nature reserves in the country and in May it has a spectacular carpet of bluebells which
you can admire through the railings.

The Ballot Box pub gained its strange name from a time when boatmen from the
canal used to walk to the hostelry to vote. There is a children's play area by the car park.

As you enter Horsenden Wood, see how many holes you can count in the trees.
These belong to woodpeckers, but there are many other species of birds here too, such
as treecreepers, nuthatches and spotted flycatchers. The woods themselves are a relic
of the prehistoric forest that once covered much of southern England and contain,
among the oak, hornbeams and the unusual wild service tree.

Route 12

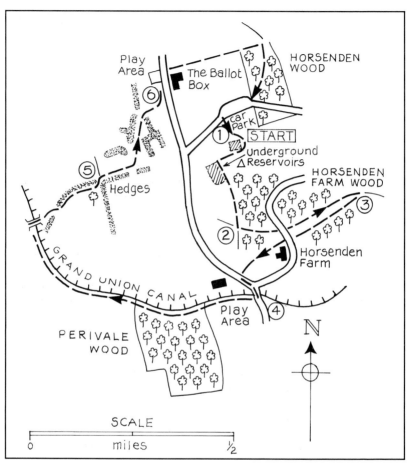

Wild Service Tree
Sorbus torminalis

Route 12

Horsenden Hill and the Grand Union Canal   2½ miles

Start

In the Council car park off Horsenden Lane North. From Greenford take the A4127 towards Harrow and, with the Glaxo buildings on your left, turn right along the A4090. After half a mile turn right along Horsenden Lane North (Greenford). The car park is signposted on the left just after the Ballot Box public house (GR 162844).

Route

1. *From the car park follow the path up a flight of steps to the triangulation point. Turn right downhill by a post where there is no tree cover along a grassy path, turning left after 75 metres to reach a flat rectangular area bordered by logs. Cross this to a gap in the hedge and follow the gravelly path downhill through a field.*

2. *Where a gravel path joins from the right and the main path goes straight on, turn left along a small muddy path. Go over a crossing path after 50 metres (noting the good climbing tree on the right) and continue, eventually veering left. The path is distinguished here by stones protruding from the soil. Within sight of the golf course turn right down a lane and after five metres take the first left-hand path into the woods. Go straight ahead until you reach the point where a parallel path runs alongside your path.*

3. *Turn right, doubling back on your direction to the lane. Cross and go straight ahead to the main road. Turn left and cross the canal by a footbridge, then turn left on to the towpath, doubling back under the bridges.*

4. *Follow the towpath (taking advantage of a children's play area and open space on the left just beyond the bridge) and after half a mile cross the canal by the wooden bridge. Follow the path for 25 metres and turn right through the hedge across a plank bridge and then left, following the hedge.*

5. *At the corner of the field, just before a solitary oak, turn left through a clear gap in the hedge across another plank bridge. Turn right and walk with the hedge on your right. Pass one small gap with a plank bridge and at the second gap in the hedge turn half-left for 70 metres to saplings where there is another bridge. Cross the next square field diagonally and go through the hedge. Turn right and cross the playing field to the road opposite The Ballot Box.*

6. *Cross the road **carefully** and just beyond The Ballot Box car park turn right along a tarmac path. Where this ends at a street turn right into the woods and take the right fork. Walk slightly uphill for 200 metres. The car park is on your right.*

Public Transport

To the south: Perivale Tube Station; 297 bus from Willesden Garage to Ealing Broadway. To the north: Sudbury Town Tube Station; 187 bus from South Harrow Station to Queens Park Station.

Refreshments

There are plenty of attractive picnic spots on Horsenden Hill, but for those who prefer it, The Ballot Box provides meals and has tables and a children's play area in its garden at the back.

A picnic in Ten Acre Wood (route 13)

Yeading Brook and Gutteridge Wood

Outline
Charville Lane – Ten Acre Wood – Gutteridge Pond – Gutteridge Wood –
Charville Lane.

Summary
A pleasant walk through woods and meadows in an oasis of farmland in Hillingdon.
Unfortunately, it is not suitable for pushchairs, but it is short enough to be attempted
by the more energetic toddler. In mid-summer it can be overgrown in parts.

Attractions
The countryside in the middle of Hillingdon is a charming remnant of a former way
of life where the fields are grazed by herds of cows and where meadows of
wildflowers blaze with colour in the summer months. Charville Lane itself is of
ancient origin, possibly even a prehistoric route from Uxbridge. It was used by cattle
drovers who wanted to avoid paying toll at Yeading Lane

In the 1860s the local manor was bought by Sir Charles Mills, who closed many
of the rights of way, including Charville Lane, in order to use the land for pheasant
shooting. Naturally, this did not go down too well with nearby residents and to
celebrate Queen Victoria's Jubilee in 1897 a trio of local men set forth with suitable
tools to reopen the Lane. With the blessing of the police, they re-bridged the stream
and cut a path through the plantation that had grown up on the other side. Then they,
and a thousand others including the Chairman of Uxbridge Council and a local
magistrate, walked along the path to reinstate it.

In keeping with this tradition, the London Wildlife Trust, in association with the
Council, are opening up paths and building bridges and stiles to enable people to enjoy
the woods and meadows. Ten Acre Wood, which you walk through first, is full of
blackberries for those who come in the autumn. Look out for the red campion which
is in flower for most of the summer.

As you cross the farmland towards Gutteridge Wood make a detour to the right
to see the pond, recently installed on the site of an old sewage works. There are
spectacular dragonflies here and you will see plenty of butterflies in the surrounding
meadows, including the common blue and the meadow brown.

Gutteridge Wood itself is very old: Rocques map shows that it was well established
in 1754. Mainly oak, but with ash, hazel and elm, it is an excellent habitat for birds.
You can see different species of tit and warbler and along the river there are
kingfishers, distinguished by their shrill, highpitched whistle. Muntjac deer live here
too, but they are not often seen as they are very shy.

Refreshments
There are none nearby, but you can find places to picnic in the meadows.

Route 13

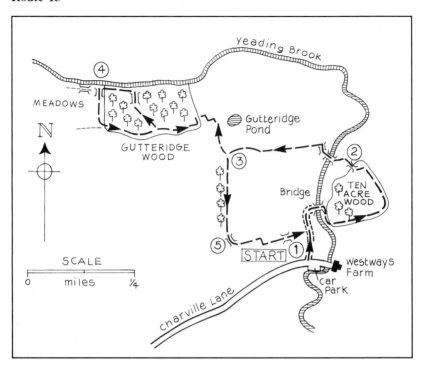

The local branch of the London Wildlife Trust installing a bridge

Route 13

Yeading Brook and Gutteridge Wood 2 miles

Start

At the car park in Charville Lane. Take the A4020 (Uxbridge Road, Uxbridge, Hayes) from Hillingdon to Hayes and turn left up Pole Hill Road. It turns sharply right and becomes Charville Lane. At a mini-roundabout turn left and where the lane ends at Westways Farm park on the right (GR 097836).

Route

1. *Cross the lane from the car park and go through a metal gate and pedestrian entrance. Follow the track, which turns right and crosses the stream by a wooden bridge. Turn right and after 20 metres leave the road and turn left along a footpath that follows the edge of the wood. Keep the boundary of the wood on your right until you reach a wooden bridge over a ditch on your right.*

2. *Cross it, following the Hillingdon Trail sign and walk slightly left across the meadows (which may be overgrown in summer). Turn right at another signpost to cross a bridge, then immediately after a stile go over another bridge and turn left along a path bounded by a barbed-wire fence on the right. Climb a stile to cross a field entrance. Continue over another stile, over two bridges, then go right to follow another path bounded by a barbed-wire fence and a hedge. Go over two more stiles and then over a third which takes you into open land. The path meanders, but keep the field boundary on your left until you see a stile.*

3. *Turn right to join a path coming from the stile, still following the Hillingdon Trail signs. Cross the meadow, passing a sign to Gutteridge Pond (turning right to see it) then follow the zig-zagging wire fence until you reach a stile into Gutteridge Wood on the left. Climb over and cross the bridge, then turn left following the path until you see a stile and gate on the left. Turn right here, by the Hillingdon Trail signpost and continue until you join a path by another signpost. Turn right and cross a brick bridge to follow the path which runs along the edge of the main brook.*

4. *Just before the path crosses a wooden bridge turn left, with a ditch on your right. Cross another bridge to come out into meadows. Go straight ahead, keeping the edge of the wood on your left. (This may be overgrown.) When you join a path at the far side of the wood turn left, and continue, now just within the boundary of the wood once more, until you reach the bridge and stile you came in by. Retrace your steps to 3, this time going straight ahead over the stile to walk between wire fences to the end of the field.*

5. *Go over the stile and then over a bridge. Turn left along the edge of the field. Turn the corner and then go left through a gap in the hedge. Follow the path straight*

ahead, and at a stream go left to cross it by a bridge. Continue along the path until you reach the gravel track. Turn right and retrace your route to the car park.

Public Transport
Bus routes 207A, Uxbridge circular and 195 from Ealing Hospital to Charville Lane Estate both stop in Charville Lane.

The Slough Arm of the Grand Union Canal

Little Britain Lake and the Grand Union Canal

Outline
Little Britain Lake − Slough Arm − Grand Union Canal − River Colne − Little Britain Lake.

Summary
This is an ideal walk for those who like water. The route circles a lake, follows the towpaths of two canals and finally returns by way of a river. It can be very muddy, even in summer and the river stretch (½ mile) is unsuitable for pushchairs.

Attractions
The River Colne forms part of a network of parallel rivers linked by flooded gravel pits that run from Rickmansworth down to the Thames at Staines and which have recently been made into the Colne Valley Park. Little Britain Lake is one such gravel pit, now home to many different fish, including perch, chub, pike and trout, and as the rivers and canals are well stocked too, the area is popular with anglers.

As you climb down to the towpath of the Slough Arm of the Grand Union Canal, have a look at the stone pillar under the bridge. It is a coal duty post and marked the place where coal bound for London was liable for tax. The Slough Arm was completed in 1882, and was the last canal to be built in England. It is five miles long and was used to carry bricks from Langley Brick Works as well as bringing refuse from London to fill in the gravel pits. Note the aqueduct that carries the canal over Fray's River. Made of cast iron, it was needed to keep the canal above the surrounding land to prevent it from taking water from local rivers and so decreasing the power available for the mills. You can see the remains of a mill on Fray's River if you drive up Old Mill Lane but, ironically, the mills have disappeared, while the canals are very much in use!

This quiet stretch of canal provides a habitat for many different plants and birds and you may be lucky enough to see water voles emerging from their holes low down in the banks. Where the Slough Arm joins the main Grand Union Canal there is much more activity. Narrow boats are moored along the side and on the right, just before you go under Packet Boat Lane, is a dock, the terminus for the Paddington Packet Boat service. In 1801 the Grand Union Canal Company set up a passage and parcel service between Paddington and Uxbridge, pulled by four horses, but it was short lived, ending in 1806. Further on, past an open space with welcome seats, is Cowley Lock, the first lock for 20 miles.

Refreshments
Quackers Restaurant and The Turning Point near the start of the walk offer refreshments and The Shovel which has a Harvester's Restaurant, makes a pleasant canal-side break halfway round.

Route 14

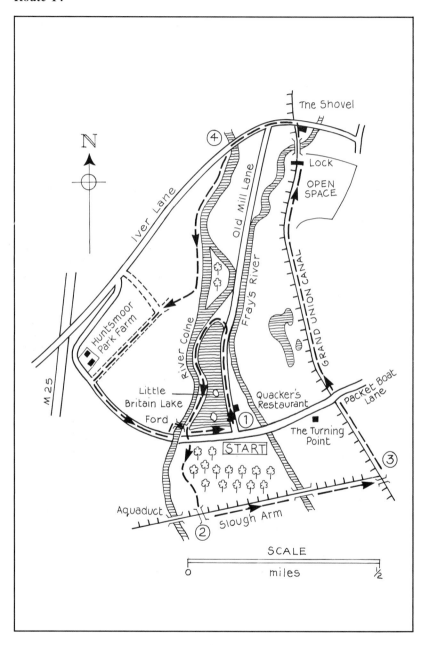

The Shovel

Lock

OPEN SPACE

N

Iver Lane

Old Mill Lane

Fray's River

GRAND UNION CANAL

River Colne

Huntsmoor Park Farm

M 25

Little Britain Lake

Ford

Quacker's Restaurant

Packet Boat Lane

START

The Turning Point

④

①

③

Aquaduct

Slough Arm

②

SCALE

0   miles   ½

Route 14

Little Britain Lake and the Grand Union Canal 3½ miles

Start

In Packet Boat Lane, opposite the entrance to Old Mill Lane. Take the A408 (High Street, Cowley, Uxbridge) from West Drayton to Uxbridge and turn left at the Paddington Packet Boat pub into Packet Boat Lane (GR 050811).

Route

1. *Cross the road and walk on a path between Old Mill Lane and Little Britain Lake, continuing round the lake past picnic tables at the end, and finally along a path with the lake on one side and the River Colne on the other. (This circuit can be done at the end of the walk if you prefer.) Leave the lake by a metal gate, passing a footbridge on the right, and go straight ahead along a muddy path with water on your right.*

2. *Cross over the bridge and turn left down large steps to the towpath of the Slough Arm of the Grand Union Canal, then turn right along the path. Continue to a bridge over the main Grand Union Canal, cross it with care, as there are large gaps in the rails, and again turn left down to the towpath and then right.*

3. *Walk along the towpath for a mile and a half, under two road bridges and past an open green with seats. When you pass Cowley Lock the path climbs up to a road. Turn left along the road over the canal, past the entrance to Old Mill Lane (you may wish to cross the busy road to use the footpath on the other side). Immediately after the bridge over the River Colne turn left down wooden steps along a path marked 'Colne Valley Way'.*

4. *Continue with the river on your left, keeping right at a concrete platform on the left and crossing a tributary by a concrete bridge. Ignore an incoming path from the right and keep straight ahead along a made up track until you cross a stile on to the road.*

5. *Turn left and follow the road to the river, then turn left along the river bank for a few metres to a footbridge. Cross it and turn right to follow the edge of Little Britain Lake back to the car.*

Public Transport

Bus route 222 from Hounslow to Uxbridge goes along High Street, Cowley.

Cowley Lock on the Grand Union Canal

Route 15   **2½ miles**

Langley Park

Outline

Billet Lane car park − Treal Farm − Langley Park Lake − rhododendron gardens − Billet Lane car park.

Summary

Langley Park is a pleasant combination of open land and trees, semi-formal gardens and an arboretum. Part of the walk follows the field boundaries out of the Park along an old Saxon earth wall and back past the lake − so remember your bread for the ducks.

Attractions

The avenue of trees at the start of the walk dates from the mid-18th century when Capability Brown designed the grounds of Langley House. There is a fine arboretum on the right where the children may like to play hide and seek.

After the woods the path skirts the parkland along a very unusual raised ridge which is believed to be the remains of a Saxon boundary.

When you turn into the field that leads you past the lake enjoy the view of Langley House. The original drive used to run this way to Windsor and it was known as Marlborough Way, after the third Duke of Marlborough who built the present house in 1755. In 1976 there was a severe drought and as the lake dried little fires started to break out in the cracked mud. Investigation revealed that the Polish army who had their headquarters in the house in the Second World War and dumped unused ammunition in the lake when the war ended. They had also buried it in other parts of the park and it took the army two years to make the grounds safe.

Although Langley House belongs to a private company it is maintained in 18th-century style and all new furniture − even cabinets for VDUs − have to be period pieces. It was rebuilt in 1755 by Stiff Leadbetter but on the left are the original 1603 red brick buildings which housed the laundry, slaughter house, brewery, dairy and kitchens. The elegant clock tower with its bell was very necessary to summon staff scattered over the whole estate. From 1788 the house passed from the Duke of Marlborough to Sir Robert Bateson Harvey, a descendant of Oliver Cromwell, and it remained in the family until 1945 when it became the property of Buckingham County Council.

From the platform in the rhododendron garden you can look across to Windsor Castle. Where the seats are now was once a 50-foot tower built in 1866 by the second Sir Robert Harvey in memory of his father. It was considered unsafe and demolished in 1959 but locals can remember climbing up the inside in pitch darkness when they were children.

Route 15

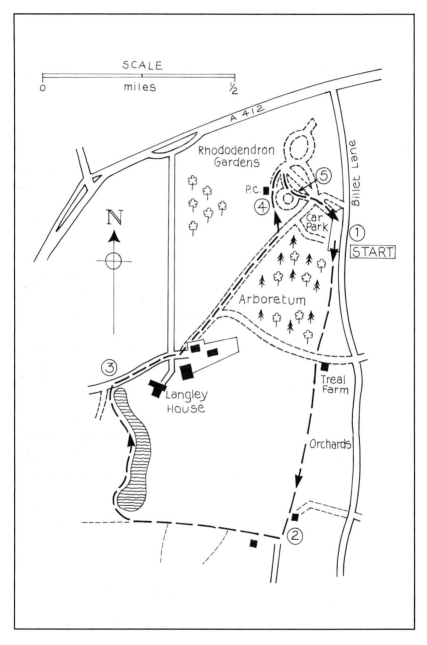

Route 15

Langley Park   2½ miles

Start

At the car park in Billet Lane. Take the A4007 from Uxbridge to Slough. At a roundabout with the Crooked Billet on the left take the A412 to Slough. Turn left down Billet Lane (signposted to Langley Country Park) and the car park is ⅔ mile on the right (GR 016823).

Route

1. *Facing the information panel at the car park turn left down the broad grassy avenue with redwood trees on the right. Go through the fence by a gate and cross a track to follow the footpath into woodland straight ahead. Turn right over a stile on to an enclosed path with fields on the right and eventually climb over another stile. Continue straight ahead passing a footpath to the left and following the boundary wall of Park Cottage on the left.*

2. *Where the path joins a road on the left, turn right over a stile and follow the path with fields on the right and a farm building on the left. After a wicket gate pass two footpath signs to the left and go over a stream by wooden planks. Turn right at the first stile on the right with a sign stating that this is a permissive footpath to Langley Park. Follow the path round the left (west) side of the lake.*

3. *Where the lake ends go through a gate and turn right along the road past Langley Hall on the right. Cross the main entrance drive and take a track that goes half-left, passing the buildings of an Environmental Studies Centre on the right. At the first fork keep left and follow the track until you reach a second fork where you turn left to reach the toilet building.*

4. *From the toilets, turn half-right through a gate into the rhododendron garden. Follow the path ahead until you reach a junction with a sign directing you to the toilets. Turn right here and continue to a gravel path. Turn left and, after a few yards, turn left on to a terrace with seats and a good view of Windsor Castle.*

5. *At the back of the terrace go through the gap in the yew hedge and turn right. Pass a seat on the right and go over a crossing path. Follow the main path, ignoring turnings to right and left until you join another path. Turn right, and the car park is visible on your left.*

Public Transport

Bus routes 458 and 558 for Uxbridge to Slough stop at the roundabout by the Crooked Billet pub (called Five Points). It is one mile from the start of the walk.

Refreshments

There are plenty of places to picnic. Calves Lane 'Pick Your Own' Farm is signposted in Billet Lane and sells ice cream.

The lake in Langley Park

Black Park

Outline
Black Park Lake – Five Points Corner – Pinewood Studios – Black Park Lake.

Summary
If you like trees, this is the walk for you. Sandy tracks take you through mixed woodland, conifer plantations and the occasional open space as well as past the Pinewood Film Studios. Black Park Lake has a swimming section and there is an excellent children's play area behind Centenary Lodge. This walk is suitable for pushchairs with an alternative route in wet weather.

Attractions
Aptly named Black Park because of its density of trees, the original forest was used for hunting, but in the 1840s the third Duke of Marlborough who owned Langley Park employed veteran soldiers to plant pine trees along the edges of the lake. Legend has it that these were arranged in the troop formation of the battle of Blenheim, but this can't be confirmed because none of the old trees remains. In 1841 a new sawmill was opened at Rowley Farm to replace the original one in Black Park and water from the lake was used to power it. Now the lake is used for swimming, model boats and fishing.

The forest is still a commercial timber plantation, but, in 1976, a devastating fire broke out and in a single afternoon on August 26, 48 acres were destroyed. You can still see the blackened trunks to the south-east of Five Points Corner. New trees were to be planted to replace those lost, but when the deforested areas showed signs of reverting to natural heathland, a rare habitat today, it was decided to manage these patches of heath to retain the wealth of wildlife that is found there.

In the rest of the Park felled timber is replaced with deciduous as well as evergreen trees which creates a friendlier environment for birds and animals and especially for the insects they feed on. In the open space at Five Points Corner, there is a profusion of wild flowers, including the common spotted orchid, ragged robin and scarlet pimpernel. Tempting though they are, remember not to pick them! Watch out for adders and grass snakes as they bask in the sun.

The Pinewood Studios lie along the eastern edge of the Park and you may occasionally come across a camera crew in the woods – many a well-known film has been shot here.

Leaving the Studios and returning along the imposing avenue of trees to Centenary Lodge you can see Corsican pine, which have dark trunks, and Scots pine which are yellow towards the top. Squirrels do a lot of damage here and you may spot a tree that has had its bark stripped off near the ground and teeth marks in the wood where the sap has been eaten.

Route 16

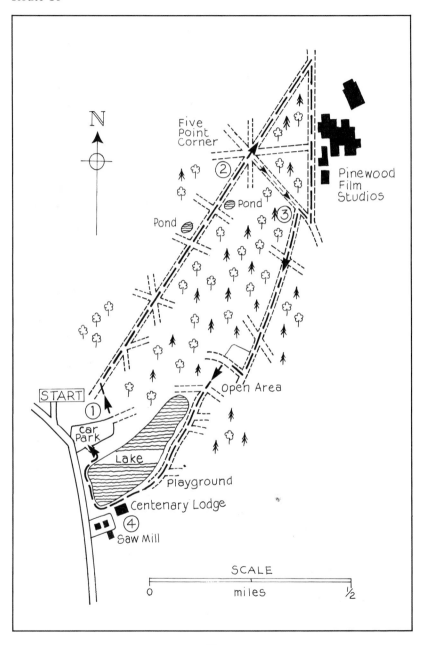

N

Five
Point
Corner

②

Pinewood
Film
Studios

Pond

Pond

③

④

START

①

Car
Park

Open Area

Lake

Playground

Centenary Lodge

Saw Mill

SCALE

0   miles   ½

Route 16

Black Park

2½ miles (Wet weather alternative for pushchairs)

Start

At Black Park car park. Follow the A4007 from Uxbridge to Slough and at a roundabout with the Crooked Billet on the left take the A412 to Slough. After a mile turn right along Black Park Road and the car park is on the right after a further mile (GR 006833).

Route

1. *At the far end of the car park go through the wooden gate just before the picnic tables and turn left along a gravelly path. Keep on until you reach a track. Turn right and continue straight ahead, passing an open area on your right. Where there is a crossing of six paths maintain direction. At the next crossroads continue straight ahead with birch trees on the left and mature larches on the right. After passing a pond on the right of the track you will soon reach Five Points Corner, indicated by a map on a post.*

2. *There are actually eight paths in all. Walk straight ahead, passing the map post on your left, and where your path forks take the right-hand track. Ignore a crossing track and continue until you reach the edge of the forest. Turn right here and continue with the Pinewood Studios on your left, passing two right-hand tracks. Just beyond the second of these the path broadens out into a grassy ride; at the end of this take a right-hand track and after 20 metres turn left (where the alternative route joins).*

3. *Go straight ahead over another crossroads where there is a map on a post and along an avenue of tall trees. Continue over the next crossing track past another map until you come to an open space suitable for picnics and games. Turn right along the edge of this with the wood on your right, going slightly downhill, and then up into another space with a timber construction on your right. Don't follow the path into the woods. Instead turn left along the edge of the trees until you reach a crossroads and can see the lake ahead. Go straight ahead with the lake on your right and follow the shore to Centenary Lodge where there is a swimming area and an adventure playground.*

4. *From Centenary Lodge continue round the lake and take any left-hand path which will lead you back to the car park.*

Wet weather alternative for pushchairs

At Five Points Corner take the second path on the right and continue over a crossing path to join the route at 3.

Public Transport

Bus routes 458 and 558 go from Uxbridge to Slough, stopping at the roundabout by the Crooked Billet (called Five Points) but it is two miles to the start of the walk.

Refreshments

A kiosk at the Centenary Lodge sells a range of snacks, and there are picnic tables, both here and in the woods.

By the edge of Black Park Lake

Useful information

Walks in order of difficulty

None of the walks in this book is strenuous for an able-bodied adult, but I have graded them according to distance and to the amount of concentration needed to follow the route. A canal walk, for example, is easier to follow than one through woods.

Easy walks

Route 9 — River Wey and Wey Navigations (not suitable for pushchairs)
Route 12 — Horsenden Hill and the Grand Union Canal (not suitable for pushchairs)
Route 14 — Little Britain Lake and the Grand Union Canal (all but half a mile suitable for pushchairs)
Route 15 — Langley Park (not suitable for pushchairs)
Route 16 — Black Park (suitable for pushchairs)

Moderate walks

Route 3 — Wimbledon Common (intrepid pushchair owners only)
Route 4 — Bushy Park and the Woodland Gardens (suitable for pushchairs)
Route 5 — Hampton Court and the River Thames (suitable for pushchairs)
Route 6 — Windsor Great Park (suitable for pushchairs)
Route 7 — Runnymede and Cooper's Hill (not suitable for pushchairs)
Route 8 — Chobham Common (not suitable for pushchairs)
Route 13 — Yeading Brook and Gutteridge Woods (not suitable for pushchairs)

More difficult walks

Route 1 — Richmond Park (intrepid pushchair owners only)
Route 2 — Marble Hill Park, Ham Lands and the Thames (short route suitable for pushchairs)
Route 10 — West End and Esher Commons (not suitable for pushchairs)
Route 11 — Osterley Park (pushchairs possible through Park itself)

Maps

The following 1:25,000 Pathfinder sheets cover the routes and can be a useful supplement to the book as they show extra detail including houses and field boundaries. All the walks are found in the area defined by the 1:50,000 sheet 176, West London. In addition I have included road names using the London A-Z street map where appropriate.

Route 1 — 1174 (TQ 07/17) Staines, Heathrow Airport and Richmond and 1175 (TQ 27/37) Wimbledon and Dulwich
Route 2 — 1174 (TQ 07/17) Staines, Heathrow Airport and Richmond
Route 3 — 1175 (TQ 27/37) Wimbledon and Dulwich
Route 4 — 1174 (TQ 07/17) Staines, Heathrow Airport and Richmond and 1190 (TQ 06/16) Weybridge, Hampton Court and Esher
Route 5 — 1190 (TQ 06/16) Weybridge, Hampton Court and Esher
Route 6 — 1173 (SU 87/97) Windsor
Route 7 — 1173 (SU 87/97) Windsor and 1174 (TQ 07/17) Staines, Heathrow Airport and Richmond
Route 8 — 1189 (SU 86/96) Bracknell and Ascot
Route 9 — 1190 (TQ 06/16) Weybridge, Hampton Court and Esher
Route 10 — 1190 (TQ 06/16) Weybridge, Hampton Court and Esher
Route 11 — 1174 (TQ 07/17) Staines, Heathrow Airport and Richmond
Route 12 — 1158 (TQ 08/18) Hillingdon and Wembley
Route 13 — 1158 (TQ 08/18) Hillingdon and Wembley

Route 14 – 1158 (TQ 08/18) Hillingdon and Wembley
Route 15 – 1158 (TQ 08/18) Hillingdon and Wembley
Route 16 – 1158 (TQ 08/18) Hillingdon and Wembley

Travel information

London Transport, including buses and underground. Tel. 071-222 1234.
For free local guides and timetables. Tel. 071-371 0247.
River boat information. Tel. 0839 123 432
British Rail Network Southeast. Tel. 071-928 5100.
For further information on the many different bus companies operating in West London and surrounding counties contact the local tourist office.

Tourist Information Centres

London Tourist Board, 26 Grosvenor Gardens, SW1W 0DU. Tel. 071-730 3488.
Aylesbury, County Hall, Walton Street. Tel. 0296 382308;.
Guildford, The Undercroft, 72 High Street. Tel. 0483 444007.
Harrow, Civic Centre, Station Road. Tel. 081-424 1103/2/1.
Hounslow, 24 The Treaty Centre, Hounslow High Street. Tel. 081-572 8279.
Richmond, Old Town Hall, Whittaker Avenue. Tel. 081-940 9125.
Twickenham, The Atrium, Civic Centre, York Street. Tel. 081-891 7272.
Windsor, Central Station, Thames Street. Tel. 0753 852010.

Useful phone numbers

British Waterways (for leaflets, guides, etc). Tel. 0923 226422.
Colne Valley Groundwork Trust. Tel. 0895 832662.
Countryside Commission (South East). Tel. 071-831 3510.
London Canals Project. Tel. 071-289 9897.
London Natural History Society. Tel. 071-952 7711.
London Walk Information, c/o Lee Valley Regional Park Authority
  Countryside Centre. Tel. 0992 713838.
London Wildlife Trust. Tel. 071-278 6612.
National Trust. Tel. 071-222 9215.
Online Leisure Services (for information on all aspects of leisure in the London area). Tel. 071-222 4640.
The Ramblers' Association. Tel. 071-582 6878.

Places to visit

Museums

West London has many local museums displaying information and artefacts from the vicinity and though small these can contain a wealth of information. As some are staffed by volunteers you should ring to check opening times.
Brooklands Museum, Brooklands Road, Weybridge, Surrey. Tel. 0932 857381.
Chertsey Museum, 33 Windsor Street, Chertsey, Surrey. Tel. 0932 565764.
Egham Museum, Literary Institute, High Street, Egham, Surrey. Tel. 0344 843047.
Elmbridge Museum, Church Street, Weybridge, Surrey. Tel. 0932 843573.
Kingston Museum and Heritage Centre, Wheatfield Way, Kingston upon Thames, Surrey. Tel. 081-546 5386.

Surrey Heath Museum, Knoll Road, Camberley, Surrey. Tel. 0276 686252, Ex 284.

Richmond Museum, Old Town Hall, Whittaker Avenue, Richmond, Surrey. Tel. 081-332 1141.

Wimbledon Windmill Museum, Windmill Road, off Parkside, Wimbledon. Tel. 081-788 7655.

Chiltern Open Air Museum, Newland Park, Gorelands Lane, Chalfont St Giles, Bucks, HP8 4AD. Tel. 0494 871117. *45 acres of parkland and a collection of historic buildings. Has a cafe.*

Kew Bridge Steam Museum, Green Dragon Lane, Brentford, Middlesex. Tel. 081-568 4757. *A Victorian waterworks housing large steam pumping engines, in steam at weekends although museum open daily.*

London Canal Museum, 12/13 New Wharf Road, Kings Cross, N1 94T. Tel. 071-713 0836. *Contains information on London's canals, including history and wildlife.*

Musical Museum, 368 High Street, Brentford, Middlesex. Tel. 081-560 8108. *A fine collection of automatic musical instruments. Opportunity to hear as well as see these inventions.*

Church at West End (route 10)

Historic Houses

Chiswick House, Burlington Lane, Chiswick, W4 2RP. Tel. 081-995 0508. *Palladian style house with landscaped gardens.*

Ham House, Ham Street, Ham, Richmond, Surrey. Tel. 081-940 1950. *Late 17th-century house and gardens.*

Hampton Court Palace, East Molesey, Surrey, KT8 9AU. Tel. 081-977 8441. *Built in 1514 by Cardinal Wolsey it has magnificent apartments and grounds, including a maze, historic 'real' tennis court and vine.*

Marble Hill House, Richmond Road, Twickenham, Middlesex, TW1 2NL. Tel. 081-892 5115. *Palladian villa built for the Countess of Suffolk, Henrietta Howard. Collection of early Georgian paintings, furniture and prints.*

Orleans House, Riverside, Twickenham, Middlesex, TW1 3DJ. Tel. 081-892 0221. *Houses art exhibitions including a fine collection of local views.*

Osterley Park, Osterley, Isleworth, Middlesex. Tel. 081-560 3918. *Robert Adam interior in the 18th-century house and spacious grounds with lakes.*

Syon Park, Brentford, Middlesex, TW8 8JP. Tel. 081-560 0881/3. *18th-century house and gardens landscaped by Capability Brown. Has a Motor Museum and Butterfly House which are both very popular with children.*

Windsor Castle, Windsor, Berkshire. *The doll's house is a popular feature for children.*

Narrow boat on the Grand Union Canal (route 12)

Paddle boat on the River Thames at Runnymede (route 7)

Gardens

Kew Gardens. Tel. 081-940 1171. *Plenty of space for children and greenhouses for a rainy day. Has a cafe.*

Brent Lodge Park, Church Road, Hanwell, W7. *Includes a collection of small animals.*

Claremont Gardens, Portsmouth Road, Esher. Tel. 0372 53401. *Attractive landscaped gardens with lake and tea room.*

Royal Horticultural Gardens, Wisley, Woking, Surrey, GU23 6QB. Tel. 0483 224234. *Beautiful garden with cafe.*

Savill Garden, Wick Lane, Egham, Surrey. *Provides a pleasant diversion in Windsor Great Park. Includes a cafe.*

Terrace Gardens, Richmond. *Attractive views over the Thames and squirrels for the children to feed. Has a small cafe.*

Farms

Hounslow Urban Farm, Fagg's Road, Feltham, TW14 0NB. Tel. 081-751 0850. *Selection of farm animals and playground.*

Calves Lane 'Pick Your Own' Farm, Billet Lane, Langley Park, Iver, Slough, Bucks, SL0 OL4. Tel. 0753 652727. *Sells ice cream.*

Garsons 'Pick Your Own' Farm, Winterdown Road, Esher, Surrey, KT10 8LS. Tel. 0372 464389. *Many different fruit and vegetables to pick, large garden centre, farm shop and restaurant.*

There are many other places to visit in London and information about these, including leisure centres and swimming pools, can be found at the local tourist office.

THE FAMILY WALKS SERIES

The publishers welcome suggestions for further titles in this series; and will be pleased to consider manuscripts relating to Derbyshire from new or established authors.

Scarthin Books of Cromford, in the Peak District, are also leading second-hand and antiquarian booksellers, and are eager to purchase specialised material, both ancient and modern.

Contact Dr D.J. Mitchell, 0629-823272.